The Perfect Pick-Up!

Is yours tall, dark and handsome, like the Double Chocolate Chunk Muffins on page 4? Or super sweet and a little bit nutty, like the Apple Cinnamon Crunch Muffins on page 10?

Maybe your stud muffin is tan and lovable with a sweet disposition, like the Pumpkin Muffins with Vanilla Icing on page 12. Or maybe you just want steady and reliable, like The Best Bran Muffins on page 8.

No matter what you want in a stud muffin, this book will hook you up with plenty of drool-worthy photos and crave-causing recipes to satisfy your hunger. Go ahead and try them all. Maybe there's more than one stud muffin for you!

Printed in the United States of America
by G&R Publishing Co.

Published By:

507 Industrial Street
Waverly, IA 50677

ISBN-13: 978-1-56383-335-9
ISBN-10: 1-56383-335-2
Item # 7034

10 Muffin-Making Tips

1. Most muffin cups should be filled about ⅔ full.

2. Fill jumbo muffin cups with about ⅝ cup of batter, fill standard muffin cups with about ⅓ cup batter, and fill miniature muffin cups with about 2 tablespoons batter. Most recipes in this book will make approximately 6 jumbo muffins, 12 standard muffins or 30 miniature muffins.

3. Grease muffin cups with nonstick cooking spray or use a paper towel that has been dipped in shortening to lightly grease each cup. If using paper liners, spray the insides lightly with nonstick cooking spray.

4. For muffins with a rounded top, grease only the bottom and halfway up the sides of each cup.

5. If some muffin cups will remain empty during baking, pour 2 to 3 tablespoons water in the unused cups to keep the pan from warping.

6. If baked muffins stick to the bottom of the muffin cup, place the hot muffin pan on a wet towel for about two minutes.

7. Watch muffins closely while baking. Miniature muffins will require a much shorter baking time than standard or jumbo muffins. To test doneness, stick a wooden toothpick in the top of a muffin. If no crumbs cling to the toothpick when pulled out, the muffins are done.

8. Mix the wet and dry ingredients together until they are just barely mixed. Too much mixing will cause loss of leavening, resulting in muffins that don't rise.

9. As soon as the batter is mixed, fill muffin cups and bake immediately.

10. Both unbaked batter and baked muffins can be frozen. To freeze baked muffins, individually wrap the baked and cooled muffins in plastic wrap and place them in a freezer bag. To freeze batter, fill the muffin tins as usual and place in the freezer until the batter is frozen. Transfer the frozen batter portions to a freezer bag. To bake, place the batter portions back in a muffin tin and allow to thaw in the refrigerator before baking as normal.

Double Chocolate Chunk Muffins

*Makes 6 jumbo muffins,
12 standard muffins or 30 miniature muffins*

Muffins

6 T. unsalted butter

4 oz. bittersweet chocolate, coarsely chopped, divided

2 C. all-purpose flour

⅔ C. white sugar

⅓ C. unsweetened cocoa powder, sifted

1 T. baking powder

½ tsp. baking soda

½ tsp. salt

1¼ C. buttermilk

1 large egg

1 tsp. vanilla extract

Miniature chocolate chips, optional

Preparation

Place an oven rack in the center position and preheat the oven to 375°.
Grease the cups of a muffin tin or fit the cups with paper liners.

In a double boiler over simmering water, combine the butter and half of
the bittersweet chocolate; stir until melted and smooth. Remove the pan
from the heat and set aside.

In a large bowl, whisk together the flour, white sugar, cocoa powder,
baking powder, baking soda and salt; set aside. In a large glass
measuring cup, whisk together the buttermilk, egg and vanilla. Pour the
liquid ingredients over the dry ingredients; add the melted chocolate.
Stir everything together quickly but gently. Stir in half of the remaining
chopped bittersweet chocolate. Spoon the batter evenly into the muffin
cups. Sprinkle the remaining chopped chocolate over the batter in each
cup. If desired, sprinkle some miniature chocolate chips over the batter
in each cup, as well.

Bake the muffins for 20 minutes or until a toothpick inserted in the
center comes out clean. Let the pan cool on a rack for 5 minutes before
removing each muffin from its cup.

Sour Cherry Muffins

Makes 6 jumbo muffins,
12 standard muffins or 30 miniature muffins

Muffins

2 C. all-purpose flour

1 C. plus 1 T. white sugar, divided

1 T. baking powder

1 tsp. salt

1 C. whole or 2% milk

2 large eggs, lightly beaten

½ C. unsalted butter, melted

1 T. poppy seeds

1 to 2 T. grated orange zest

1 C. dried red sour cherries

Preparation

Place an oven rack in the center position and preheat the oven to 400°.
Grease the cups of a muffin tin or fit the cups with paper liners.

In a large bowl, whisk together the flour, 1 cup white sugar, baking
powder and salt; set aside. In a large glass measuring cup, whisk
together the milk and eggs. Stir the melted butter, poppy seeds and
orange zest into the milk mixture.

Form a well in the center of the dry ingredients. Pour the milk mixture
into the well and fold gently until just combined. Fold in the cherries.
Spoon the batter evenly into the muffin cups. Sprinkle a little of the
remaining white sugar over the batter in each cup.

Bake the muffins for 20 minutes or until a toothpick inserted in the
center comes out clean. Let the pan cool on a rack for 5 minutes before
removing each muffin from its cup.

The Best Bran Muffins

Makes 6 jumbo muffins, 12 standard muffins or 30 miniature muffins

Muffins

1½ C. bran cereal (like All-Bran, not flakes)
½ C. boiling water
½ C. white sugar
6 T. unsweetened applesauce

1 large egg
1¼ C. whole-wheat flour
1¼ tsp. baking soda
¼ tsp. salt
1 C. skim milk
1 T. lemon juice

Preparation

Place an oven rack in the center position and preheat the oven to 400°. Grease the cups of a muffin tin or fit the cups with paper liners.

Place the cereal in a large bowl. Pour the boiling water over the cereal and let stand for 2 minutes. In a separate bowl, whisk together the white sugar, applesauce, egg, whole-wheat flour, baking soda and salt. In a large glass measuring cup, whisk together the milk and lemon juice; add to the flour mixture.

Fold the flour mixture into the softened cereal in the bowl; mix gently until just combined. Spoon the batter evenly into the muffin cups.

Bake the muffins for 15 to 20 minutes or until a toothpick inserted in the center comes out clean. Let the pan cool on a rack for 5 minutes before removing each muffin from its cup.

Apple Cinnamon Crunch Muffins

Makes 6 jumbo muffins,
12 standard muffins or 30 miniature muffins

Muffins

1 large egg, beaten

½ C. skim milk

¼ C. canola oil

2 medium tart apples, grated with the skin on

1½ C. all-purpose flour, sifted

¼ C. white sugar

2 tsp. baking powder

¼ tsp. salt

½ tsp. ground cinnamon

Topping

3 T. brown sugar

3 T. chopped walnuts

¼ tsp. ground cinnamon

Preparation

Place an oven rack in the center position and preheat the oven to 400°. Grease the cups of a muffin tin or fit the cups with paper liners.

In a large bowl, beat the egg with a whisk; stir in the milk, oil and grated apple. In a separate bowl, whisk together the flour, white sugar, baking powder, salt and ½ teaspoon cinnamon. Fold the dry ingredients into the milk mixture; mix gently until just combined. Spoon the batter evenly into the muffin cups.

In a small bowl, combine the topping ingredients. Sprinkle some of the topping over the batter in each cup.

Bake the muffins for 20 to 25 minutes or until a toothpick inserted in the center comes out clean. Let the pan cool on a rack for 5 minutes before removing each muffin from its cup.

Pumpkin Muffins with Vanilla Icing

*Makes 6 jumbo muffins,
12 standard muffins or 30 miniature muffins*

Muffins

1½ C. all-purpose flour
1 tsp. baking powder
1 (15 oz.) can pumpkin puree
⅓ C. vegetable oil
2 large eggs

1 tsp. pumpkin pie spice
1¼ C. plus 1 T. white sugar, divided
½ tsp. baking soda
½ tsp. salt
1 tsp. ground cinnamon

Vanilla Icing

1 C. powdered sugar

1½ T. milk

¼ tsp. clear vanilla extract

Preparation

Place an oven rack in the center position and preheat the oven to 350°. Grease the cups of a muffin tin or fit the cups with paper liners. Small ramekins can also be used.

In a large bowl, whisk together the flour and baking powder. In a separate bowl, mix together the pumpkin, oil, eggs, pumpkin pie spice, 1¼ cups white sugar, baking soda and salt. Fold the dry ingredients into the pumpkin mixture; mix gently until just combined. Spoon the batter evenly into the muffin cups or ramekins.

In a small bowl, combine the cinnamon and remaining 1 tablespoon white sugar; sprinkle some over the batter in each cup.

Bake the muffins for 25 minutes or until a toothpick inserted in the center comes out clean. Let the pan cool on a rack for 5 minutes before removing each muffin from its cup.

While the muffins are baking, combine the icing ingredients; stir until blended and smooth. Spoon or drizzle some of the icing over the top of each cooled muffin.

Rhubarb Buttermilk Muffins

Makes 6 jumbo muffins, 12 standard muffins or 30 miniature muffins

Muffins

- 1½ C. finely chopped fresh rhubarb
- 1 T. white sugar
- 1 C. all-purpose flour
- 1 C. whole-wheat flour
- 1 tsp. baking powder
- 1 tsp. baking soda
- ½ tsp. ground cinnamon
- ½ tsp. salt
- 1 large egg, lightly beaten
- ¾ C. brown sugar
- 2 T. canola oil
- 1 C. low-fat buttermilk
- 1 tsp. vanilla extract

Preparation

Place an oven rack in the center position and preheat the oven to 400°.
Grease the cups of a muffin tin or fit the cups with paper liners.

In a large bowl, toss together the rhubarb and white sugar; set aside.

In another large bowl, whisk together both flours, baking powder,
baking soda, cinnamon and salt. In a separate bowl, mix together
the egg, brown sugar, oil, buttermilk and vanilla. Add the buttermilk
mixture to the dry ingredients; mix until just combined. Fold in the
rhubarb. Spoon the batter evenly into the muffin cups.

Bake the muffins for 15 to 20 minutes or until a toothpick inserted in
the center comes out clean. Let the pan cool on a rack for 5 minutes
before removing each muffin from its cup.

Blueberry Streusel Muffins

Makes 6 jumbo muffins,
12 standard muffins or 30 miniature muffins

Muffins

2 C. all-purpose flour
½ C. white sugar
2 tsp. baking powder
½ tsp. baking soda
½ tsp. salt

2 eggs, lightly beaten
1 (6 to 8 oz.) carton lemon
 yogurt
½ C. vegetable oil
1 C. fresh or frozen
 blueberries

Streusel Topping

⅓ C. white sugar

¼ C. all-purpose flour

2 T. butter or margarine

Preparation

Place an oven rack in the center position and preheat the oven to 400°. Grease the cups of a muffin tin or fit the cups with paper liners.

In a large bowl, whisk together the flour, white sugar, baking powder, baking soda and salt. In a separate bowl, combine the eggs, yogurt and oil. Add the yogurt mixture to the dry mixture; mix until just combined. Fold in the blueberries. Spoon the batter evenly into the muffin cups.

In a small bowl, combine the streusel ingredients until crumbly. Sprinkle a portion of streusel over the batter in each cup.

Bake the muffins for 20 minutes or until a toothpick inserted in the center comes out clean. Let the pan cool on a rack for 5 minutes before removing each muffin from its cup.

Peanut Butter Nut Muffins

*Makes 6 jumbo muffins,
12 standard muffins or 30 miniature muffins*

Muffins

2 C. all-purpose flour
1 T. baking powder
1 C. 1% or 2% milk
2 large eggs

½ C. white sugar
½ C. creamy peanut butter
1 tsp. salt

Topping

¼ C. chopped peanuts

¼ C. miniature chocolate
chips or coarsely chopped
semi-sweet chocolate

Preparation

Place an oven rack in the center position and preheat the oven to 400°. Grease the cups of a muffin tin or fit the cups with paper liners.

In a large bowl, whisk together the flour and baking powder; set aside. In the container of a blender, combine the milk, eggs, white sugar, peanut butter and salt. Cover the blender container and process until blended and smooth, about 10 seconds. Pour the peanut butter mixture over the dry ingredients; mix until just combined. Spoon the batter evenly into the muffin cups.

Sprinkle some of the chopped peanuts and chocolate chips over the batter in each cup.

Bake the muffins for 15 to 20 minutes or until a toothpick inserted in the center comes out clean. Let the pan cool on a rack for 5 minutes before removing each muffin from its cup.

Java Mocha Muffins

*Makes 6 jumbo muffins,
12 standard muffins or 30 miniature muffins*

Muffins

3 large eggs

1 C. buttermilk

¾ C. canola oil

½ C. strong brewed coffee, room temperature

1 tsp. vanilla extract

1½ C. all-purpose flour

1¼ C. whole-wheat flour

⅓ C. unsweetened cocoa powder

1 C. brown sugar

½ tsp. baking powder

1 tsp. baking soda

½ tsp. salt

1 C. white chocolate chips

1¼ C. chopped peanuts, divided

Preparation

Place an oven rack in the center position and preheat the oven to 375°. Grease the cups of a muffin tin or fit the cups with paper liners.

In a large bowl, whisk together the eggs, buttermilk, oil, coffee and vanilla; set aside. In a separate bowl, combine both flours, cocoa powder, brown sugar, baking powder, baking soda and salt. Mix the dry ingredients into the coffee mixture; stir until just combined. Fold in the white chocolate chips and 1 cup chopped peanuts. Spoon the batter evenly into the muffin cups.

Sprinkle some of the remaining ¼ cup chopped peanuts over the batter in each cup.

Bake the muffins for 20 to 25 minutes or until a toothpick inserted in the center comes out clean. Let the pan cool on a rack for 5 minutes before removing each muffin from its cup.

Oatmeal Raisin Cookie Muffins

*Makes 6 jumbo muffins,
12 standard muffins or 30 miniature muffins*

Muffins

¼ C. butter or margarine

1 C. old-fashioned oats, divided

⅔ C. brown sugar, divided

¼ tsp. ground cinnamon

¼ tsp. ground allspice

⅔ C. water

1½ C. all-purpose flour

4 tsp. baking powder

2 tsp. wheat germ

1 large egg, lightly beaten

1 C. evaporated milk

1⅓ C. raisins

Preparation

Place an oven rack in the center position and preheat the oven to 375°. Grease the cups of a muffin tin or fit the cups with paper liners.

Melt the butter in a medium skillet over medium heat. Stir in ⅔ cup oats, ⅓ cup brown sugar, cinnamon and allspice. Heat, stirring often, until the oats are toasted and golden brown. Stir in the water and remaining ⅓ cup brown sugar; cook until slightly thickened. Remove the skillet from the heat and let cool.

In a large bowl, whisk together the flour, baking powder, wheat germ and the remaining ⅓ cup oats. In a separate bowl, whisk together the egg and evaporated milk. Form a well in the center of the dry mixture and pour the egg mixture and cooked oatmeal mixture into the center; mix until just combined. Fold in the raisins. Spoon the batter evenly into the muffin cups.

Bake the muffins for 25 minutes or until a toothpick inserted in the center comes out clean. Let the pan cool on a rack for 5 minutes before removing each muffin from its cup.

Chunky Apple Breakfast Muffins

*Makes 6 jumbo muffins,
12 standard muffins or 30 miniature muffins*

Muffins

2 C. all-purpose flour
¼ C. white sugar
1 T. baking powder
1 tsp. ground cinnamon
¼ tsp. salt

2 Fuji apples, peeled, cored
  and coarsely chopped
½ C. 1% or 2% milk
¼ C. molasses
¼ C. vegetable oil
1 large egg
1 C. raisins

Preparation

Place an oven rack in the center position and preheat the oven to 450°. Grease the cups of a muffin tin or fit the cups with paper liners.

In a large bowl, combine the flour, white sugar, baking powder, cinnamon and salt. Add the chopped apples and stir until evenly mixed. In a separate bowl, whisk together the milk, molasses, oil and egg. Add the molasses mixture to the dry ingredients; mix until just combined. Fold in the raisins. Spoon the batter evenly into the muffin cups.

Bake the muffins for 5 minutes. Reduce the oven temperature to 350° and bake the muffins for an additional 15 minutes or until a toothpick inserted in the center comes out clean. Let the pan cool on a rack for 5 minutes before removing each muffin from its cup. If desired, drizzle with Vanilla Icing found on page 13.

Orange Grove Muffins

Makes 6 jumbo muffins, 12 standard muffins or 30 miniature muffins

Muffins

1½ C. all-purpose flour

1¾ tsp. baking powder

½ C. white sugar

½ tsp. salt

¼ tsp. ground allspice

¼ tsp. ground nutmeg

⅓ C. butter or margarine

1 (10 oz.) can mandarin oranges

1 large egg, lightly beaten

1 small orange or tangerine, thinly sliced with peel still on

Preparation

Place an oven rack in the center position and preheat the oven to 350°. Grease the cups of a muffin tin or fit the cups with paper liners.

In a large bowl, combine the flour, baking powder, white sugar, salt, allspice and nutmeg. Cut in the butter with a pastry blender or two knives until crumbly. Drain and reserve the juice from the mandarin oranges. Measure the juice to equal 7 tablespoons. Add the mandarin juice and egg to the flour mixture; mix until just combined. Fold in the mandarin oranges. Spoon the batter evenly into the muffin cups.

Place one orange slice over the batter in each cup. If making miniature muffins, top each one with a mandarin orange segment.

Bake the muffins for 20 minutes or until a toothpick inserted in the center comes out clean. Let the pan cool on a rack for 5 minutes before removing each muffin from its cup.

Toffee Crunch Muffins

*Makes 6 jumbo muffins,
12 standard muffins or 30 miniature muffins*

Muffins

1½ C. all-purpose flour
⅓ C. brown sugar
2 tsp. baking powder
½ tsp. baking soda
½ tsp. salt
½ C. 1% or 2% milk
½ C. sour cream

3 T. butter or margarine, melted
1 large egg, lightly beaten
1 tsp. vanilla extract
3 (1.4 oz.) chocolate-covered toffee bars, finely chopped, divided

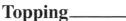

Topping

½ C. prepared white frosting
Fresh raspberries
Chocolate shavings

Preparation

Place an oven rack in the center position and preheat the oven to 400°. Grease the cups of a muffin tin or fit the cups with paper liners.

In a large bowl, combine the flour, brown sugar, baking powder, baking soda and salt. In a separate bowl, combine the milk, sour cream, butter, egg and vanilla. Add the milk mixture to the dry ingredients; mix until just combined. Fold in ⅔ of the chopped toffee bars. Spoon the batter evenly into the muffin cups.

Sprinkle the remaining chopped toffee bars over the batter in each cup.

Bake the muffins for 15 to 20 minutes or until a toothpick inserted in the center comes out clean. Let the pan cool on a rack for 5 minutes before removing each muffin from its cup.

To serve, top each cooled muffin with a dollop of the frosting. Garnish each with a raspberry and some chocolate shavings.

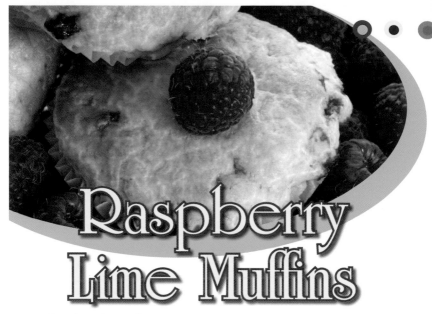

Raspberry Lime Muffins

Makes 6 jumbo muffins, 12 standard muffins or 30 miniature muffins

Muffins

2 C. all-purpose flour
2 tsp. baking powder
½ tsp. salt
½ C. butter or margarine, softened

¾ C. white sugar
2 large eggs, lightly beaten
1 tsp. vanilla extract
¼ tsp. grated lime zest
½ C. 1% or 2% milk
1½ C. fresh raspberries

Topping

¼ C. fresh lime juice

½ C. powdered sugar

3 T. white sugar

Preparation

Place an oven rack in the center position and preheat the oven to 375°. Grease the cups of a muffin tin or fit the cups with paper liners.

In a large bowl, combine the flour, baking powder and salt. In a separate bowl, cream together the butter and ¾ cup white sugar; stir in the eggs, vanilla and lime zest. Add the milk to the butter mixture. Add the butter mixture to the dry ingredients; mix until just combined. Gently fold in the raspberries. Spoon the batter evenly into the muffin cups.

Bake the muffins for 20 minutes or until a toothpick inserted in the center comes out clean; remove from oven and set aside. Preheat the broiler.

Meanwhile, combine the lime juice and powdered sugar; drizzle over the muffins. Sprinkle the remaining white sugar over the muffins and place under the broiler for 1 to 2 minutes, being careful not to let the muffins burn. Remove the muffins from the oven and let the pan cool on a rack for 5 minutes before removing each muffin from its cup.

Southern Cornbread Muffins

*Makes 6 jumbo muffins,
12 standard muffins or 30 miniature muffins*

Muffins

1½ C. cornmeal
½ C. all-purpose flour
1 T. baking powder
⅛ tsp. salt
¾ C. butter, melted

1½ C. 1% or 2% milk
2 large eggs, lightly beaten
2 T. ground flaxseed or
   additional cornmeal

Place an oven rack in the center position and preheat the oven to 375°. Grease the cups of a muffin tin or fit the cups with paper liners.

In a large bowl, combine the cornmeal, flour, baking powder and salt. In a separate bowl, whisk together the butter, milk and eggs. Add the butter mixture to the dry ingredients; mix until just combined. Pour the batter evenly into the muffin cups.

Sprinkle a little ground flaxseed or additional cornmeal over the batter in each cup.

Bake the muffins for 20 minutes or until a toothpick inserted in the center comes out clean. Let the pan cool on a rack for 5 minutes before removing each muffin from its cup.

Cheesy Sun-Dried Tomato Muffins

Makes 6 jumbo muffins, 12 standard muffins or 30 miniature muffins

Muffins

2 C. all-purpose flour

2 tsp. baking powder

1 tsp. baking soda

Salt and pepper to taste

2 T. dried basil

2 T. crushed red pepper flakes

2 T. extra-virgin olive oil

½ C. chopped green onions

8 cloves garlic, minced

2 large eggs

1 C. cottage cheese

½ C. shredded mozzarella or Parmesan cheese

1½ C. finely chopped oil-packed, sun-dried tomatoes

1¼ C. whole milk

¼ C. shredded Cheddar cheese

2 T. poppy seeds

Preparation

Place an oven rack in the center position and preheat the oven to 350°. Grease the cups of a muffin tin or fit the cups with paper liners.

In a large bowl, sift together the flour, baking powder and baking soda. Stir in the salt, pepper, basil and red pepper flakes; set aside. Heat the oil in a large skillet over medium-high heat. Sauté the green onions and garlic until softened; set aside to cool slightly.

In a separate bowl, beat the eggs until fluffy; stir in the sautéed onions and garlic. Add the egg mixture to the dry ingredients. Fold in the cottage cheese, mozzarella cheese and sun-dried tomatoes. Slowly stir in the milk; mix until just combined. Spoon the batter evenly into the muffin cups.

Sprinkle some of the Cheddar cheese and poppy seeds over the batter in each cup.

Bake the muffins for 20 minutes or until a toothpick inserted in the center comes out clean. Let the pan cool on a rack for 5 minutes before removing each muffin from its cup.

Glazed Lemon Poppy Seed Muffins

Makes 6 jumbo muffins,
12 standard muffins or 30 miniature muffins

Muffins

3 C. all-purpose flour
1 T. baking powder
½ tsp. baking soda
2 T. poppy seeds
½ tsp. salt

½ C. plus 2 T. unsalted
butter, softened
1 C. white sugar
2 large eggs
1 T. grated lemon zest
1½ C. plain yogurt

Glaze

2 T. fresh lemon juice
1 C. powdered sugar

Preparation

Place an oven rack in the center position and preheat the oven to 375°. Grease the cups of a muffin tin or fit the cups with paper liners.

In a large bowl, whisk together the flour, baking powder, baking soda, poppy seeds and salt; set aside. In a separate bowl, cream together the butter and white sugar, mixing until fluffy. Add the eggs to the creamed mixture one at a time, beating well after each addition. Stir in the lemon zest. Fold in half of the dry ingredients along with one-third of the yogurt, mixing well. Add half of the remaining dry ingredients and another one-third of the yogurt. Beat in the remaining dry ingredients and yogurt; mix until just combined. Spoon the batter evenly into the muffin cups.

Bake the muffins for 20 to 25 minutes or until a toothpick inserted in the center comes out clean. Let the pan cool on a rack for 5 minutes before removing each muffin from its cup.

Meanwhile, whisk together the glaze ingredients, adding more lemon juice as needed until the glaze is a drizzling consistency. While the muffins are still slightly warm, drizzle some of the glaze over each muffin.

Gingerbread Muffins

Makes 6 jumbo muffins, 12 standard muffins or 30 miniature muffins

Muffins

2 C. all-purpose flour
1 tsp. baking soda
1½ tsp. ground ginger
1¼ tsp. ground cinnamon
½ tsp. ground cloves
½ tsp. ground nutmeg
1 C. molasses
½ C. brown sugar
½ C. canola oil
1 C. boiling water
2 T. powdered sugar

Preparation

Place an oven rack in the center position and preheat the oven to 350°. Grease the cups of a muffin tin or fit the cups with paper liners.

In a large bowl, whisk together the flour, baking soda, ginger, cinnamon, cloves and nutmeg; set aside. In a separate bowl, mix together the molasses, brown sugar, oil and boiling water. Add the molasses mixture to the dry ingredients; mix until just combined. Spoon the batter evenly into the muffin cups.

Bake the muffins for 25 minutes or until a toothpick inserted in the center comes out clean. Let the pan cool on a rack for 5 minutes before removing each muffin from its cup. Sift powdered sugar over the muffins after they have cooled slightly.

Pistachio Muffins

*Makes 6 jumbo muffins,
12 standard muffins or 30 miniature muffins*

Muffins

1 (18.25 oz.) box yellow
cake mix

1 (3 oz.) pkg. pistachio-
flavored instant pudding mix

4 large eggs, lightly beaten

1¼ C. water

¼ C. canola oil

½ tsp. almond extract

7 drops green food coloring

¼ C. finely chopped pistachios

Preparation

Place an oven rack in the center position and preheat the oven to 350°. Grease the cups of a muffin tin or fit the cups with paper liners.

In a large bowl, combine the cake mix, pudding mix, eggs, water, oil and almond extract. Beat mixture with an electric mixer at low speed until just combined. Add the green food coloring and increase speed to medium, mixing until thoroughly combined. Spoon the batter evenly into the muffin cups.

Sprinkle some of the chopped pistachios over the batter in each cup.

Bake the muffins for 20 minutes or until a toothpick inserted in the center comes out clean. Let the pan cool on a rack for 5 minutes before removing each muffin from its cup.

Dark Chocolate Banana Nut Muffins

Makes 6 jumbo muffins, 12 standard muffins or 30 miniature muffins

Muffins

- 1 C. whole-wheat flour
- 1 C. all-purpose flour
- 2 tsp. baking powder
- 1 tsp. baking soda
- ½ tsp. salt
- ½ C. plus ⅔ C. bittersweet chocolate chips, divided
- ½ C. chopped pecans or walnuts

- ¼ C. butter, softened
- 2 large eggs, lightly beaten
- ¾ C. brown sugar
- ½ C. unsweetened applesauce
- 1 banana, mashed
- ⅔ C. buttermilk
- 1 tsp. vanilla extract

Topping

2 T. unsweetened cocoa powder
1 T. plus 2 tsp. water
1 T. vegetable oil

1 T. corn syrup
1 C. powdered sugar
Banana chips

Preparation

Place an oven rack in the center position and preheat the oven to 375°. Grease the cups of a muffin tin or fit the cups with paper liners.

In a large bowl, combine both flours, baking powder, baking soda and salt; stir in ½ cup chocolate chips and nuts. In a small saucepan over very low heat, heat the remaining ⅔ cup chocolate chips and butter until melted and smooth. Remove from the heat and let cool to room temperature. In a medium bowl, whisk together the eggs, brown sugar, applesauce, banana, buttermilk, vanilla and melted chocolate mixture. Pour the chocolate mixture over the dry ingredients; mix until just combined. Spoon the batter evenly into the muffin cups.

Bake the muffins for 20 minutes or until a toothpick inserted in the center comes out clean. Let the pan cool on a rack for 5 minutes before removing each muffin from its cup.

Meanwhile, combine all topping ingredients except the powdered sugar and banana chips. Stir the powdered sugar into the mixture until a glaze forms. Top each cooled muffin with a thin layer of the chocolate glaze and garnish each with a few banana chips.

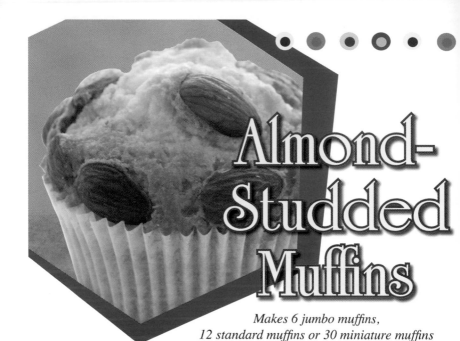

Almond-Studded Muffins

*Makes 6 jumbo muffins,
12 standard muffins or 30 miniature muffins*

Muffins

2 C. all-purpose flour
½ C. white sugar
1 T. baking powder
¼ tsp. ground nutmeg
¼ tsp. ground cinnamon
⅛ tsp. salt

½ C. chopped almonds
1 medium egg, beaten
¾ C. 1% or 2% milk
½ C. vegetable oil
½ tsp. almond extract
Whole almonds

44

Preparation

Place an oven rack in the center position and preheat the oven to 375°. Grease the cups of a muffin tin or fit the cups with paper liners.

In a large bowl, combine the flour, white sugar, baking powder, nutmeg, cinnamon, salt and chopped almonds. In a separate bowl, whisk together the egg, milk, oil and almond extract. Add the egg mixture to the dry ingredients; mix until just combined. Spoon the batter evenly into the muffin cups.

Bake the muffins for 10 minutes. Remove the pan from the oven and lightly press a few whole almonds into the batter in each muffin cup. Return the muffins to the oven for an additional 10 to 15 minutes or until a toothpick inserted in the center comes out clean. Let the pan cool on a rack for 5 minutes before removing each muffin from its cup.

Hawaiian Island Muffins

Makes 6 jumbo muffins, 12 standard muffins or 30 miniature muffins

Muffins

1⅓ C. all-purpose flour

1 C. old-fashioned oats

1 tsp. baking powder

½ tsp. baking soda

½ tsp. salt

2 medium bananas, mashed

1 C. buttermilk

½ C. brown sugar

2 T. canola oil

1 tsp. vanilla extract

1 large egg

½ C. canned crushed pineapple in juice, drained

⅓ C. sweetened flaked coconut

3 T. finely chopped macadamia nuts, toasted

Topping

2 T. sweetened flaked coconut

1 T. finely chopped
   macadamia nuts

1 T. white sugar

1 T. old-fashioned oats

Preparation

Place an oven rack in the center position and preheat the oven to 400°.
Grease the cups of a muffin tin or fit the cups with paper liners.

In a large bowl, combine the flour, 1 cup oats, baking powder, baking
soda and salt. In a separate bowl, combine the bananas, buttermilk,
brown sugar, oil, vanilla and egg. Form a well in the center of the dry
ingredients. Add the banana mixture to the dry ingredients; mix until
just combined. Fold in the pineapple, ⅓ cup coconut and 3 tablespoons
toasted macadamia nuts. Spoon the batter evenly into the muffin cups.

In a small bowl, combine the topping ingredients. Sprinkle some of the
topping over the batter in each cup.

Bake the muffins for 20 minutes or until a toothpick inserted in the
center comes out clean. Let the pan cool on a rack for 5 minutes before
removing each muffin from its cup.

Cream Cheese Delight Muffins

*Makes 6 jumbo muffins,
12 standard muffins or 30 miniature muffins*

Muffins

1 large egg, lightly beaten
¾ C. 1% or 2% milk
½ C. vegetable oil
2 C. all-purpose flour
⅓ C. white sugar

1 T. baking powder
½ tsp. salt
¼ C. brown sugar
Ground cinnamon

48

Filling

4 oz. cream cheese, softened
¼ C. white sugar
½ tsp. grated lemon zest

⅛ tsp. vanilla extract
1 large egg, lightly beaten

Preparation

Place an oven rack in the center position and preheat the oven to 350°.
Grease the cups of a muffin tin or fit the cups with paper liners.

In a medium bowl, beat together the egg, milk and oil. In a large bowl,
whisk together the flour, white sugar, baking powder and salt. Add the
egg mixture to the dry ingredients; mix until just combined and set aside.

In a small bowl, combine the filling ingredients; mix well and set aside.

Spoon the prepared batter evenly into the muffin cups, filling each about
half full. Spoon 1 teaspoon of the filling over the batter in each cup.
Top the filling in each cup with a little more batter. Sprinkle some of
the brown sugar and cinnamon generously over the batter in each cup.

Bake the muffins for 20 to 25 minutes or until the muffins are light
golden brown. Let the pan cool on a rack for 5 minutes before
removing each muffin from its cup.

Chocolate Chip Muffins

*Makes 6 jumbo muffins,
12 standard muffins or 30 miniature muffins*

Muffins

1½ C. all-purpose flour
⅓ C. white sugar
¼ C. brown sugar
½ tsp. baking powder
½ tsp. baking soda
½ tsp. ground cinnamon
½ tsp. salt

2 large eggs
½ C. unsalted butter, melted
   and slightly cooled
½ C. 1% or 2% milk
1 tsp. vanilla extract
1 C. semi-sweet chocolate
   chips
Powdered sugar

Preparation

Place an oven rack in the center position and preheat the oven to 375°. Grease the cups of a muffin tin or fit the cups with paper liners.

In a large bowl, whisk together the flour, white sugar, brown sugar, baking powder, baking soda, cinnamon and salt. In a separate bowl, beat the eggs. Stir in the butter, milk and vanilla. Add the egg mixture to the dry ingredients; mix until just combined. Fold in the chocolate chips. Spoon the batter evenly into the muffin cups.

Bake the muffins for 20 minutes or until a toothpick inserted in the center comes out clean. Let the pan cool on a rack for 5 minutes before removing each muffin from its cup.

Sift powdered sugar generously over the cooled muffins.

Sweet Carrot Muffins

Makes 6 jumbo muffins,
12 standard muffins or 30 miniature muffins

Muffins

1 C. raisins
2 C. warm water
2 C. all-purpose flour
1 T. baking powder
2 tsp. baking soda
1 tsp. salt

1 tsp. ground cinnamon
4 eggs, lightly beaten
1 C. vegetable oil
¾ C. brown sugar
3 C. shredded carrots

Frosting

1 (8 oz.) pkg. cream cheese, softened
¼ C. butter, softened
1 C. powdered sugar

½ tsp. vanilla extract
Chopped walnuts, cashews or pecans

Preparation

Place an oven rack in the center position and preheat the oven to 350°. Grease the cups of a muffin tin or fit the cups with paper liners.

Place the raisins in a small bowl and cover with the warm water; let soak while preparing batter.

In a large bowl, whisk together the flour, baking powder, baking soda, salt and cinnamon. In a separate bowl, combine the eggs, oil and brown sugar. Add the egg mixture to the dry ingredients; mix until just combined. Fold in the carrots. Drain the water from the raisins and fold the raisins into the batter. Spoon the batter evenly into the muffin cups.

Bake the muffins for 20 to 25 minutes or until a toothpick inserted in the center comes out clean. Let the pan cool on a rack for 5 minutes before removing each muffin from its cup.

In a medium bowl, combine all frosting ingredients except the chopped nuts. Once the muffins have cooled, top each with some of the frosting. Sprinkle chopped nuts over the frosting.

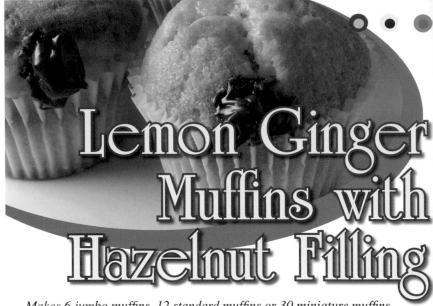

Lemon Ginger Muffins with Hazelnut Filling

Makes 6 jumbo muffins, 12 standard muffins or 30 miniature muffins

Muffins

2 C. all-purpose flour
2 tsp. baking powder
½ tsp. baking soda
½ tsp. salt
½ tsp. ground ginger
Juice of 1 large lemon

2 large eggs
1 C. plain yogurt
⅔ C. white sugar
½ C. sunflower oil
1 tsp. vanilla extract
¾ C. chocolate hazelnut
    spread, like Nutella

Preparation

Place an oven rack in the center position and preheat the oven to 375°. Grease the cups of a muffin tin or fit the cups with paper liners.

In a large bowl, whisk together the flour, baking powder, baking soda, salt and ground ginger. In a separate bowl, combine the lemon juice, eggs, yogurt, white sugar, oil and vanilla. Add the egg mixture to the dry ingredients; mix until just combined. Spoon the batter evenly into the muffin cups.

Bake the muffins for 20 minutes or until a toothpick inserted in the center comes out clean. Let the pan cool on a rack for 5 minutes before removing each muffin from its cup.

Put the hazelnut spread in a pastry bag with a long icing tip used for injecting. Once the muffins have cooled, press the tip into the top edge of a muffin. Squeeze the pastry bag while slowly drawing the tip up and out. Repeat with remaining filling and muffins.

Banana Streusel Muffins

*Makes 6 jumbo muffins,
12 standard muffins or 30 miniature muffins*

Muffins

2 C. all-purpose flour
1 C. white sugar
1 tsp. baking powder
½ tsp. salt
½ tsp. baking soda
¼ tsp. ground cinnamon

2 large eggs
1 C. sour cream
¼ C. butter or margarine, melted
2 medium bananas, mashed
1 C. miniature chocolate chips

Streusel Topping

¼ C. white sugar
3 T. all-purpose flour
¼ tsp. ground cinnamon

2 T. butter or margarine
¼ C. miniature chocolate
chips

Preparation

Place an oven rack in the center position and preheat the oven to 375°.
Grease the cups of a muffin tin or fit the cups with paper liners.

In a large bowl, whisk together the flour, white sugar, baking powder,
salt, baking soda and cinnamon. In a separate bowl, beat the eggs.
Whisk in the sour cream, butter and mashed bananas. Add the banana
mixture to the dry ingredients; mix until just combined. Fold in 1 cup
chocolate chips. Spoon the batter evenly into the muffin cups.

In a small bowl, combine all streusel ingredients, except the
¼ cup chocolate chips. Cut in the butter until crumbly. Sprinkle some
of the streusel topping and some of the chocolate chips over the batter
in each cup.

Bake the muffins for 20 minutes or until a toothpick inserted in the
center comes out clean. Let the pan cool on a rack for 5 minutes before
removing each muffin from its cup.

Strawberry Muffins

Makes 6 jumbo muffins, 12 standard muffins or 30 miniature muffins

Muffins

2½ C. plus 2 T. all-purpose flour

¾ tsp. salt

1 T. baking powder

¾ C. white sugar

½ C. canola oil

1 large egg, lightly beaten

¾ C. 1% or 2% milk

1½ C. small or chopped large strawberries, divided

Place an oven rack in the center position and preheat the oven to 375°. Grease the cups of a muffin tin or fit the cups with paper liners. Small ramekins can also be used.

In a large bowl, combine the flour, salt, baking powder and white sugar. In a separate bowl, beat together the oil, egg and milk. Add the oil mixture to the dry ingredients; mix until just combined. Fold in 1 cup strawberries. Spoon the batter evenly into the muffin cups or ramekins.

Place some of the remaining strawberries over the batter in each cup.

Bake the muffins for 20 to 25 minutes or until a toothpick inserted in the center comes out clean. Let the pan cool on a rack for 5 minutes before removing each muffin from its cup.

Metric Conversion Chart

Abbreviations

C. = cup	qt. = quart	mL = milliliter
T. = tablespoon	gal. = gallon	F = Fahrenheit
tsp. = teaspoon	lb. = pound	C = Celsius
oz. = ounce	g = gram	
pt. = pint	L = liter	

Weights (mass)

½ oz.	15 g
1 oz.	30 g
3 oz.	90 g
4 oz.	120 g
8 oz.	225 g
10 oz.	285 g
12 oz.	360 g
16 oz. (1 lb.)	450 g

Oven Temperatures

250°F	120°C
275°F	140°C
300°F	150°C
325°F	160°C
350°F	180°C
375°F	190°C
400°F	200°C
425°F	220°C
450°F	230°C

Baking Pan Sizes

Pan Size	Size (in/ qt)	Metric Volume	Size (cm)
Baking or Cake Pan (square or rectangle)	8 x 8 x 2	2 L	20 x 20 x 5
	9 x 9 x 2	2.5 L	23 x 23 x 5
	8 x 12 x 2	3 L	30 x 20 x 5
	9 x 13 x 2	3.5 L	33 x 23 x 5
Loaf Pan	4 x 8 x 3	1.5 L	20 x 10 x 7
	5 x 9 x 3	2 L	23 x 13 x 7
Round Layer Cake Pan	8 x 1½	1.2 L	20 x 4
	9 x 1½	1.5 L	23 x 4
Pie Plate	8 x 1¼	750 mL	20 x 3
	9 x 1¼	1 L	23 x 3
Baking Dish or Casserole	1 quart	1 L	–
	1½ quart	1.5 L	–
	2 quart	2 L	–

Volume Measurements (dry)

⅛ tsp.	0.5 mL
¼ tsp.	1 mL
½ tsp.	2 mL
¾ tsp.	4 mL
1 tsp.	5 mL
1 T.	15 mL
2 T.	30 mL
¼ C.	60 mL
⅓ C.	75 mL
½ C.	125 mL
¾ C.	175 mL
1 C.	250 mL
2 C. (1 pt.)	500 mL
3 C.	750 mL
4 C. (1 qt.)	1 L

Volume Measurements (fluid)

1 fluid oz. (2 T.)	30 mL
4 fluid oz. (½ C.)	125 mL
8 fluid oz. (1 C.)	250 mL
12 fluid oz. (1½ C.)	375 mL
16 fluid oz. (2 C.)	500 mL

Dimensions

1/16 inch	2 mm
⅛ inch	3 mm
¼ inch	6 mm
½ inch	1.5 cm
¾ inch	2 cm
1 inch	2.5 cm